To Haiti
With Love

MARYSE A. NELSON

ISBN: 978-0-6151-4044-5

Printed in the United States of America.

To my beloved Mark, Maya and Shana for your love and patience. I dedicate these pages also to all Haitians who have not forgotten and diligently labor for better days.

Contents

Acknowledgments

Many wonderful people contributed to this project. I offer my sincerest thanks to:

Nancy Joy Aurelus—for your unconditional support and love. You make my heart smile.
Victoire (Mammy Croix) Clermont, Croyance Aurelus, Elida and Esteve Gay—for your fundamental teachings and unquestionable love, I'll forever be grateful.
Lissade and Isemene Aurelus—For your parental guidance and all of your sacrifice.
Esperance and Bernadette Aurelus—For your love and understanding.
My folks in New York and Laboule: Joel and Judy Aurelus, Kerry, Jude, Mark, and Josh Aurelus, Jean-Baptiste and Marie Gay, Albert and Francine Clermont, Immacula, Leocal, Lionel, Bernadette, Suzette, Albert, Daniel, Miriam, Kenol, and Jean-Guibert Clermont, Leonie Metayer, Ketlie St. Surin, Carline Jean-Jacques, Schiller Etienne, Elicin and Alourdes Pyram, Agiluste Exceus, Sauveur Louissaint, Jean-Robert Gervain, Wilther and Maryse Lundy.
My Florida family: Philip Aurelus, David and Kike Aurelus, Bertholin Gay, Roosevelt and Monique Gay, Bertho and Sherlyne Gay, Jeff and Michael Jean-Baptiste, Nicole Jean-Michel, Joseph and Louise Myrthil, Justin and Odette Bonny, Kathyann and Eriberto DeJesus, Serge and Lourna Leger, Andrea Dumornay, Jean Jacques and Eliane Noel, and Marie Fung.

To Fequiere Cesaire for your love and generosity.

The greatest thanks of all to my awesome God for strength, endurance and wisdom!

Haiti Dearest,

It's been a while since we've seen each other. The last time I saw you I promised that I would make an effort to visit more often. I have not kept that promise. There just never seemed to be a right time to make the trip. Reported chaos and frightening news about you kept me, and many others, away. I longed for your company but I found it safer to wait. Do not believe, for an instant, that I have abandoned you. Though you have not seen me, I think of you all the time.

I have to be honest. The last time I saw you, I was quite saddened by your appearance. You were not the way I left you only fifteen years before. I will not ask about your health. I have heard many things. Every now and then a brother or sister comes back with news of you. I have a sense of how you are.

I have heard of the devastation that has come upon you. Often you appear in our newspapers or on our evening news. I barely recognize the ghastly depictions of you. Your photogenic days seem to be over. Your best profiles—and I remember them well—are never shown.

I have heard of the many ways you have been mistreated. There has been news of the unrest and the conflicts you have had to endure. It sounds as if you have ceased to fight. Battered and disrespected by your very own, your legs seem to have grown weary beneath the weight of your despair.

I know that you feel forsaken by some of us, whom you fought very hard to raise and protect. Though we once fed from the milk of your bosom, and while your blood continues to flow though our veins, many of us have decided to forget you. Some betray you while others deny you entirely.

My dearest, you should see some of your children. I wish you could witness the ridiculous twisting of their tongues, professing to be children of your distant neighbors. They prefer to adopt stolen identities rather than cherish their natural heritage.

I know that you cry constantly. You see, I've become a mother since we last saw each other. I think that puts me in a better position to understand part of your grief. It must be heartbreaking to watch your children leave and never look back. The abuse you suffer at the hands of those who remain must be equally devastating. My heart is heavy when I think about the rejection you endure.

I know you cry from embarrassment. How elegant I remember you to be! And yet, I am told you were truly your best before I was even born. Among all of your neighbors and sisters, you were crowned queen—you were the pearl. You were envied and people flocked in great number to be near you, to admire your beauty, to bask in your warmth, to have a taste of you, to be awed by your fertile womb.

Today the pearl has tarnished. Those who used to

praise you now point fingers and you are the object of their derision. You have become disheveled and unkempt. You have won the title: "Poorest in the Western Hemisphere." My intention is not to help you wallow in grief, but you must know that my heart aches. You must know that I understand.

I remember your stories of bravery and fortitude. I learned how you nurtured and trained strong, dedicated and valiant heroes to defend you—and you did not stop there. You naturally participated in every battle with threatening mountains, climate, forests and terrains. You were a force to be reckoned with and you became the first to proclaim independence. How amazingly awesome your history is!

It is difficult to accept that you are the same Haiti you were so many years ago. Your present condition bears a pitiful contrast to your rich history. You have been unrightfully and undeservedly brought down to your knees.

Years of wrongdoing have rendered you paralyzed and now "ti frekan ak ti tintin"[1] you would not even have bothered with in your glory days, have openly become your bullies.

Though you cry, Haiti dearest, do take courage. Wipe your tears for, truly, we have not all forgotten you. I know it is difficult to tell, but some of your children have been fighting diligently on your behalf. Not all of us have left without any desire to return. Not all of us have left without a plan.

Oh darling, you would be so proud to see how many of us have kept all of your teachings close to our hearts. Because of you, we are masters of self-preservation, self-reliance and respect. If you could only see the number of your children sitting in high places all over the world! You have birthed professionals of unsurpassed caliber and extraordinary poise. I know you are not yet reaping the fruits of their labor, but do take heart. We have not all forgotten you and as insulting as it is of me to ask you to be more patient, please do bear with us.

You see, those of us who truly care, hear your every teardrop. Every blow you suffer is like a dagger into our very own hearts—and from deep within your belly, we instinctively bear witness to the collective plea of your heroes, our ancestors, begging us to hold you up, to sustain you, to breathe life into you, to not allow you to die. The bones of every slave who came to know freedom and of every man and woman who fought on your behalf are angrily rattling within you. They will not rest in peace until you are again the Haiti we were once proud of.

In closing, please know that although the situation seems bleak, there is still hope. Even in the ashes, there is hope. My love for you is that of a child for its mother— totally unconditional. No matter how you look, no matter how you are, you are mine. I claim you. I adore you. In my eyes, you are still the precious, priceless pearl. My grandmother used to say: "Depi tet nou poko koupe, n-espere met chapo!"[2]

You still breathe. There is hope.

With all my love,

Maryse

---

[1] *Individuals or entities of little significance*

[2] *A Haitian proverb with the literal meaning: "As long as we have not been decapitated, we can be hopeful of wearing hats."*

Introduction

I began this project several years ago. To a great extent, I felt that I had accomplished some major milestones and was actually nearing the end of the first few chapters of my life dedicated to "the self". I felt a burning desire to change course. I wanted to begin paying my dues to the country of my birth and to a world that had sustained me for so many years.

My desire to help generated several creative ideas, the least elaborate of which was the concept of this book. Although I had several plans to choose from, I remained indecisive for many months—primarily due to limited resources. Then, one day, the best option became crystal clear to me. I was watching the Oprah Winfrey Show when she made the following statement: *"Most people think they have to do a great big thing to change the world, but one small positive act can go a long way. It can tremendously impact someone's life."* This was in reference to a mother who showed great compassion to a little girl—her son's playmate. They were neighbors but unbeknownst to the mother and son, the little girl's parents were strongly addicted to drugs. They would smoke or inject the drugs into their bodies as their young daughter watched in dismay. The girl could not be taken care of properly and she lived in deplorable conditions.

The young lady ended up taking charge of her life, even overcoming homelessness when she left home as a teenager. She became a well acclaimed Harvard graduate. That day, on Oprah, she expressed her gratitude to her friend's mother for having served her the only nutritious meals she remembered having as a child. She was thankful for the times she played with her friend, because it was only then she felt normal. She said: "*I don't know what would have happened to me if I did not have you and your son for friends.*"

The small act of regularly providing the young girl with a hot dinner and companionship had a profound impact. It was a vital contribution to everything that catapulted her from a deplorable, homeless, existence straight into the prestigious arms of Harvard University and into a future no less promising.

It is in the context of that story that I came to a great realization. It was not necessary to wait for the best of times to consider making a contribution. I did not have to have all the free time in the world. I did not have to wait for the children to be in college.

My more creative ideas were too complicated and

required manpower I was not sure I would be able to get. They required sacrifice, commitment and generosity in great abundance. After careful consideration, I decided to begin with the tiny act of writing this book. However small a deed it might seem, I am dedicating the hours spent putting these pages together to my Haiti. It is my hope that it will be well-received for the sake of our wounded country.

My parents sent for me, in 1980, to come live with them in the United States. Up until that point, I had enjoyed a very normal, happy, childhood made possible by my grandparents, the money my parents sent to them for my care, and other wonderful close relatives who played pivotal roles in my life. At ten years old, I was not even aware of the Haitian culture I had absorbed. I could never have predicted that, in the future, it would become the filter through which my every behavior, decision and thought would be sifted.

As I grew older and became more and more assimilated into the American way of life, I began to feel a certain sense of responsibility to my first home. The more America adopted me, the stronger the natural connection I felt to my place of birth. I began to care very deeply. I often felt guilty when I compared my new way of life with what I had left behind.

I made a promise to myself that I would someday join the movement of creating a better Haiti. However, like many well-meaning Haitians abroad, my "someday" never seemed to come. The reason was simple: I had convinced myself that my contribution would have to be sophisticated. Any action would have to be considerably big in order to effectively counteract our huge national situation.

The story on the Oprah Winfrey show gave me a brand new perspective. It made me realize that it was possible to start without the accompanying marching band.

In deciding to write this book I realized that the

main focus would have to be on solving Haiti's problems. After all, a solution to Haiti's problems has always been the primary concern of our people. "Haiti needs a solution" is a phrase that still resonates from the microphones of great public orators to the walls of barber shops all over the world. When we hear those words from the time we first begin to make logical sense of them well into our adulthood, an impression forms in the mind that this solution is perhaps an impossibility—and the search for it, a huge, burdensome, undertaking. Some of us dream this solution to be a major, explosive, event that results in Haiti's instant recovery.

The more I live, the more I hear about this solution that no power on earth has yet been able to bring to light and the more rational I become, the more I realize that we have allowed ourselves to remain in reverie while we rapidly nosedive. Some of us find ourselves stuck in an emotional quandary of wanting to give, yet, we are convinced that our best may never be good enough. We have plainly become frozen by the perceived enormity of the task before us. We become lethargic at the very thought of it, yet, we continue to falsely hope for this solution full of promise and deliverance to literally fall from the sky.

When I think about our circumstance as a people, I find myself pondering several questions: What if this long awaited solution was not really to come as a great anticipated event, but rather, was a whole entity comprised of millions of tiny components? And what if within every one of us was the full capability of being responsible for one of those parts? What if by doing just one small thing well within our capability, limitations and available resources, each one of us was actually able to help weave together what could ultimately become "our solution"? And what if the greatest truth of it all is that every single one of those small acts is as equally powerful and necessary as the grand total of them all?

To Haiti With Love, is the beginning of my small contribution—my first attempt to bring to light simple truths that hopefully will lead to action. I am very humble in this undertaking and in no way assume that my vision is better than anyone else's. I do believe, however, that if we can look at ourselves in the mirror and honestly evaluate every blemish, we can begin to move forward. If we can be honest with ourselves long enough to establish a clear and realistic starting point of reference, we can begin to formulate plans of action. We can watch them take form and come to life as we start to reverse the effects of our painful plunge.

My philosophy is simple: We can all give in proportion to what we have—but we can all give. We owe it to ourselves, we owe it to our children, we owe it to our ancestors, and we owe it to Haiti.

PART ONE

Why we Fall

1

Falling

Haiti cries because we are falling. She mourns the disappearance of an effective and efficient society as she casts an eye on our immediate environment. She experiences hard evidence of our downfall on many different levels. For example, there is a child whose entire future is denied, not by his own idleness but by a society that tells him he is of the wrong color, born to the wrong parents and belongs to the wrong social class. As time passes, the young man comes to believe that he is indeed limited and inferior. His daily survival is a struggle as he encounters fierce resistance with every effort to better himself. He is humiliated by those belonging to the right social class and suffers dearly at their hands. With no support and no hope for a miracle, he surrenders to a force greater than his own. He grows up and creates wrong children of his own, the pattern continues and we continue to fall as a people. The contribution he could have potentially made to his country will never be known.

There is a young woman whose dreams of becoming a nurse, a doctor, a judge, or perhaps a lawyer will never be realized. She sits in despair as she remembers parental eyes that were once loving and full of pride. She also remembers poverty. She recalls innocent promises she made to herself: "*I will be the one to succeed. I will be the one to get my family out of this predicament.*" She looks at herself now, worn beyond her years. Injustice has taken its toll on her. She really did her best, but that knowledge bears no consolation.

She thought she could face the world and the world would have compassion. Instead, she discovered cruel realities of monsters with angelic faces, of people anxiously waiting to take advantage of her innocence. Her society made it clear that her only competitive advantage was in selling body and soul. Innocently she took that to be a fair tradeoff for her family's wellbeing. After years of abuse and hitting brick walls, she had to accept defeat. She had to return home with children she alone could not care for— her reward for daring to dream. She cries, as do her parents, as does Haiti—and we continue to fall as a people.

There is a young man of thirty years or so who has trouble coping with his reality. As a boy, he could not get enough of his books and he excelled in school. He completed his studies with high honors and all the professors told him if anyone was going to make it, it would be him. Against all odds, he completed engineering school and his mind went wild with ideas of the many projects he would work on to elevate his people and his country.

He sits now, behind the wheels of an old taxi cab and at the end of the day sees no fair reward for his hard labor. He is told he is one of the lucky ones—at least he is doing something. Although he has abandoned all notions of working as an engineer, he fights an internal battle. His projects have been laid to rest but his mind has become a mortal enemy. An entity in itself that cannot be suppressed or taught to become uncreative, his mind is congested with plans and designs and proposals that will never see the light of day. He has no outlet for those mental productions and he lives in dire frustration. As Haiti lies desperately in need of innovative engineers, the young man is busy driving a cab and suppressing the inventive output of his mind. His society tells him that in spite of ability, preparation and willingness to learn, he can only advance if he is friends with people in high places.

We continue to fall as greed, selfishness and envy cloud our vision. Some of our greatest men and women who are respected and educated people of high social status, in reality, are vampires of society kept alive and well only by the blood of the innocent. Our falling is vividly evident in corrupt men of the cloth and of the law. It is equally evident in rich and arrogant criminals who shamelessly prostitute our country.

We fall because fear and cowardice create indifference. Many people shun public service and responsibility because with it comes personal risk and heartache. Some do not even fulfill their personal obligations to loved ones left behind. They turn deaf ears and close their eyes to the plight of their people.

In our falling, we have welcomed low self-esteem or feelings of inferiority, idleness, negative attitudes, fear of criticism and fear of accountability. We have forgotten how to effectively communicate with each other. We have neglected the mental and emotional needs of our children. We have embraced indifference and too many of us are proud to openly reject our country.

We continue to fall. This is a fact. It is also a fact that if we make a collective decision to stop falling, we can slowly accomplish just that.

2

Self-Esteem and Inferiority Complex

In graduate school I read a wonderful passage on self-esteem. The book was *Organizational Behavior*, and the author, Robbins, described self-esteem as the degree to which individuals either like or dislike themselves. Another way of looking at it is to determine how we would rate ourselves. It is where we would place ourselves, for example, on a scale of zero to ten.

People with low self-esteem often are very shy; feel helpless in many situations; do very poorly in social areas;

allow themselves to be led by others while offering very little resistance (even when they know they should); feel inferior to most people; are not initiators of conversation or projects; lack self confidence; are not very good public speakers; and finally, have an external locus of control.

An external locus of control is defined, by Robbins, as believing that one's life is being controlled by the actions of others or by outside forces. Individuals with an external locus of control neither take credit for their accomplishments nor accept blame for their mistakes.

Low self-esteem leads to many problems. People become unwilling to take risks. The fear factor becomes so great, that they refuse to step out of their comfort zones. They have no self-reliance and put their trust, faith, and hope on other people—people who could never really benefit them as they themselves could if they ever tried. Their lack of social grace, caused by low self-esteem, makes it almost impossible for them to effectively network with other individuals from whom they could greatly benefit. They are afraid to initiate action because the fear of rejection is so great.

Individuals with low self-esteem find no reason to pursue education. Instead of pursuing careers and becoming more knowledgeable, they live their lives magnifying the ill effects of racism, unjust systems and other societal sins. They allow themselves to be molded and defined by outside forces while they sit and watch.

As a people, we struggle with the issue of self-esteem. Given our current state of affairs, sometimes it is admittedly difficult to feel good about ourselves. We should understand, however, that our present situation in no way defines who we are as a people. Rather, it is indicative of faux pas combined with other external blows. We are not unlike some of the homeless people we encounter in America. Many are former doctors, university professors, lawyers, judges, and so forth. For various reasons, they find themselves in deplorable circumstances. When strangers come upon those people they automatically dispel them as vagrants. However, anyone who might have previously known those individuals would still hold them in reverence and bear testimony to the people they once were. Although their present state of being evokes pity, their past contributions are still undeniably valid. They are people of great worth to whom terrible things have happened.

We have made mistakes and many terrible things have happened to us. We are far from *being* our situation. Though our streets are littered with garbage, we know that we are some of the cleanest people in the world. To this day, our poorest country folks upon rising in the morning must first sprinkle water on the dirt floor of their hut, then sweep before they can begin to think about eating breakfast. We are still hard-working, we are still intelligent and we are still strong.

We are not worthless. Every strong person has

faltered at one time or another. When a boxer is knocked out during a match, it does not always mean that he is weak and lacks determination. His downfall only means that whoever he was up against got the better of him. However, the inner drives that prepared him for years and got him into the boxing ring remain intact. We have suffered greatly and at the moment we are lethargic. However, our basic value systems and inner strengths are still intact. The minute we start to believe we are our situation, we set ourselves up to continue to fall.

Low self-esteem has caused us to confuse assertiveness with disrespect and confidence with arrogance. I have come across many Haitians who are not able to claim equal status with even some of their co-workers. Making eye contact still takes a great effort. We were raised in a culture where it was considered a sign of disrespect to maintain eye contact with one's elders—especially during a confrontational exchange. However, we have to come to terms with the progressive nature of the world and the environment in which we live. Nowadays, keeping one's head down or failing to make eye contact during a conversation, in many cultures, is an automatic surrender of position and acceptance of inferiority.

Individual low self-esteem amounts to a greater national condition and we continue to fall.

3

Why We Should Care

I remember not too long ago being part of a discussion about Haiti. I was at the home of a client who actually used to vacation there many years ago. Whenever I visit him, we always end up deep in conversation about a place we both love. It was really nothing out of the ordinary when his nurse, who also happened to come by, found us reminiscing about places we were both familiar with in Haiti.

The nurse was no stranger to me. She was also Haitian and we had communicated on several occasions both on a personal and professional level. Yet, it did not take very long for me to realize how much of her I really did not know. It only took one phrase out of her to change my mood from one of sweet nostalgia to another of pure sadness and frustration. What she shared that day, unfortunately, represents the feeling of many Haitians.

"As for me," she casually stated, *"I don't want to remember anything about Haiti. I got nothing from that country and now I don't give a damn if it falls off the face of the earth!"* Blasphemy! I wanted to scream out, but instead, I remained quiet and listened carefully as our client eloquently responded and defended a country not even his own.

I have tried very hard to come to terms with the possible reasons the nurse might have had for making such a strong statement. Perhaps it was out of fear that she might be placed in the same category as the rest of those God-forsaken Haitians. Perhaps it was out of fear that she might be subject to the same humiliations we face, or better yet, that she might be made to share our blame. Whatever the reason, it is difficult for me to accept that Haitians just do not care. It is plainly unnatural because to not care is to watch one's mother doubled over in pain and to say: "To heck with her! It makes no difference if she lives or dies."

Every reason for not caring can be brought to the table but at the end of the day, they remain nothing more than lousy excuses. I have heard from people who were thrown out of the country or had to escape to save their lives. I have heard the stories of many who suffered the most agonizing treacheries in Haiti and yet, their love for her has not changed. They are able to sift through all of the mess and realize that though circumstances and people are often to blame, the country itself seldom is. If those brave individuals pray every day for a better and stronger Haiti—

the same place where perhaps they experienced their darkest days—how am I to understand the shaky stand of those who can only judge the country based on how well they were served?

The Haitian who openly professes to not care has many problems, the very least of which is selfishness. He is the Judas who betrays his own mother yet lurks in the dark waiting for a chance to feed from her carcass. He is the one who always criticizes and yet never lifts a finger to help. He is the coward hiding behind a façade of indifference only to shun responsibility. He knows very well the meaning of 'give me' but never asks: "How may I help?" He is boastful, arrogant, thinks himself superior and enables us to keep falling.

Because we are children of Haiti, at this point in time there ought to be an aching, instinctual pull on our heartstrings. There ought to be an honest desire to want to help and there ought to be an intense, guilty, nagging felt by anyone who is able to but fails to do something. Haiti is

not just an unfortunate birthplace and to say we do not care

is not only unnatural, it is downright blasphemous.

4

The Root of all Evil

Our inability to put money in its proper place is another reason we fall. Some people will do anything to acquire and keep money. For those individuals, family, health, moral values and ethics are all secondary to the almighty dollar.

In general, society tends to use money as the meter stick by which success is measured. We learn at a very early age that our main goal in obtaining a good education

is to be able to land a great job and make "lots of money."
Many parents want their children to become doctors and
lawyers not necessarily for the good they will do, but
primarily for the financial rewards. Furthermore, people
with money often acquire titles that facilitate a muscular
social stance.

It would be ridiculous to suggest that money is not
important. We all know the difference an extra dollar
makes in our lives. We create problems, however, when we
cross the line that separates ambition and healthy
competition from greed and ruthlessness; when we go
beyond what is humanely acceptable in our quest for
money; when we reach the point where we do not really
care whether the next guy literally lives or dies; when we
experience no guilt whatsoever, in taking a poor man's
entire world and making it only a fraction of our own
possessions; when we make people work until they are
lethargic and pay them not the equivalent of their labor, but

just enough to eat that day—just enough to keep them coming back like drug addicts to their dealers.

We have a problem with money when we have no conscientious reprimand for committing robbery of our very own home. The uncontrollable love of money has made us conspirators in the plot to bring our own country to its knees in the open sight of an international audience.

When resources are limited and basic necessities of life are not provided for, certain behaviors may emerge that violate the rules of society. For instance, we can understand if a man acts against his moral values and steals a loaf of bread to feed a hungry child. We cannot say we condone the action, but at least we understand. For such an act, we are able to make ethical exceptions.

The greater crime against society and one that is really difficult to understand, is the man who has plenty but will still rob just to amass more. There are many wonderful people who have been blessed materially and are doing everything in their power to help our country. At the same time, there may be just as many who do not care to sacrifice anyone in their way to have more in their pocket. Where resources are ample and people behave in such a way, we have to conclude that greed is at the very core of their actions.

I discussed self-esteem in the previous chapter but this issue of money brings us back to that subject. A lethal combination is a person with low self-esteem who has money. The money serves no other purpose than to compensate for his shortcomings. This person does anything to obtain and keep his money not for its inherent value, but for its substitutive property. Qualities and great character are not necessary for that individual to possess because his money is always at the forefront. Removing his money from him is to render that person nude to the world with every flaw overtly exposed.

As we make money the almighty ruler of our lives

and as we stop at absolutely nothing in its pursuit, we focus only on ourselves, completely miss the bigger picture and we continue to fall.

5

Yo

Yo is a little word in the Haitian Creole. Simply translated, it has the exact meaning as the pronoun *they* in English. I believe if anyone ever decided to research the most widely used word in the Haitian language, *yo* would probably win by a landslide. Although the word is used properly as a pronoun, many times it is employed in an abstract sense, where the subjects it replaces seldom exist.

As a small child, every time I found myself in

trouble, I would immediately blame it on *yo*. Most of the time, my plans did not work—my grandmother was the Sherlock Holmes of our town.

The practice of using *yo* as a culprit is one that continues well into adulthood. The older we get, the less we are required to actually identify *yo* and we begin to reference the word as if it were an individual entity—an intangible, abstract conception of our minds responsible for our every misfortune. For instance, *yo* gets blamed for initiating and spreading gossip, for not doing things well, for not allowing people to live the way they should and the list goes on and on. There are always named individuals credited for positive deeds. *Yo* often gets all the credit for everything that is negative.

Yo is extensively blamed for our national crisis. We tend to use it as a scapegoat. As trivial an issue as this might appear to be at first thought, a deeper examination reveals a tremendous psychological truth: if we can mentally eliminate any direct link between ourselves, individually, and the current state of our country, the pill becomes a lot easier to swallow. In other words, *yo*, and never ourselves is to blame. In essence, we are able to not only shift all sense of responsibility away from us, but we also gain a sense power and superiority over *yo* as we position ourselves to become critics. *Yo* does not have the problems we have; *yo* does not face the obstacles we do; if only we had the time or resources, we would do a much better job than *yo*. Psychologically, we transfer all sense of guilt and responsibility from ourselves to *yo* and we become a thorn on the sides of those who dare to step out and make a difference.

As we blame *yo* for our problems, we seem to forget that the fate of our country rests in our hands. We forget that, however burdensome it is, the task of improving Haiti is primarily ours. We fall as a people because we are afraid of this responsibility and we are not ready to accept the blame for our current situation.

It is not always easy to accept blame and hold ourselves personally accountable. Many of us have not thought about it enough to have established a connection between our actions and the state of our country. Consider Ronald, a hard-working Haitian living in the United States. How in the world can we ask Ronald to partly hold himself responsible for poverty in Haiti? It seems insane at first as the connection between the two is not readily observable. However, if we consider that for pennies a day, Ronald could make a great contribution in the life of another person living in Haiti, the thought behind the suggestion begins to emerge. Although it would not really seem fair to say that Ronald alone is responsible, it is definitely safe to suggest that, on a broader scale, many Ronalds who do have the opportunity to help but fail to do so are part of the problem.

The simple act of helping one person impacts his

entire community. When we help one person, we allow and empower that individual to touch others in his immediate surrounding. A nation is a collection of communities, so the moment we enable a person to positively impact one of those communities, we have already made a great national contribution.

The concept of contributing in such a manner is barely a new one. We hear about this strategy every day and most people do not have trouble with the idea. The obstacle to overcome is the part of initiating the act and remaining committed to it. When Ronald waits for *yo* to begin the act, notice the state we find ourselves in.

Our Diaspora has a responsibility. As a member of this group, I think we should be held to higher accountability simply because we have had the opportunity to travel outside of our country and experience first hand the methods of more advanced societies. There is a wealth of knowledge present in this group that has yet to benefit our country. The person who comes to America and works as a floor sweeper becomes very good at what he does and is knowledgeable about all aspects of keeping a floor clean. For instance, this person is an expert in the operation and usage of floor cleaning equipment, in the effectiveness of different cleaning products, in the comparison of different floor surfaces as they relate to safety, climate, etc...This is information that is of vital necessity to our country but I would venture to say that whereas this individual has no problem with performing this task in America, he would take issue with doing it in Haiti. Sweeping the floor in Haiti? That's for people who have no better option, that's for people who have never traveled. That's for *yo* to do.

It is this very attitude that keeps us behind because people who are well positioned and equipped to make a difference fail to do so. For one reason or another we keep waiting for someone else to pick up the load and come to our rescue.

I used the example of a floor sweeper purposely to emphasize the positive we can obtain from what people generally consider to be a menial job. Those of us who know better understand that there is no such thing as a menial job. Although it lacks glamour, the floor keeper's job is necessary and therefore important. Imagine the difference that can be made by all members of the Haitian Diaspora—a group rich in experience and drive! We are specialists in hotel maintenance and management, factory work, transportation services, law, medicine, health services, food services, agriculture, business management, marketing, commercial art, journalism, communications, etc... We can literally change the face of our country just by stepping out and giving a little of ourselves, by taking responsibility and by refusing to leave our most precious work to *yo* to accomplish.

I offer this suggestion especially in the context of our country: Let every time we are prompted to use the word *yo*, we instead replace it with the pronoun *I*. Let us shift all responsibility back to us and away from *yo*. If we are all doing what we can to help, we will be able to individually accept blame as well as praise.

On the door of my office, I have a little sign posted. It was given to me in 1994 by a wonderful woman named Nydia. Nydia was the Office Manager at an agency for which I worked. The little sign is quite simple, but I have always found a world of meaning in its message and that is the reason many years later, it is still hanging on my door. It reads as follows:

This is a story about three people named Everybody, Somebody, and Anybody. There was an important job to be done and Everybody was asked to do it. Everybody was sure Somebody would do it. Anybody could have done it, but nobody did it. Somebody got angry about that because it was Everybody's job. Everybody thought Anybody could do it but nobody realized that Everybody wouldn't do it. It ended up that Everybody blamed Somebody when nobody did what Anybody could have done.

6

What Will People Say?

"A life spent making mistakes is not only more honorable,
but more useful than a life spent doing nothing"
—George Bernard Shaw

I remember growing up in Haiti speaking our native Creole among friends and family while learning formal French in school. My first introduction to the fear associated with failure came when in class, one day, I mispronounced a French word and the entire class erupted in laughter. Although I was always first or second in class, the shameful feeling I experienced that day affected my entire educational experience in Haiti. It impeded me from participating in class many times when I should have. I never again wanted to be laughingstock of my peers.

I came to Brooklyn in 1980 and was immediately enrolled in the sixth grade, in Mrs. Safran's class at P.S. 100. I did not understand a word of English and making it through that first year of school was one of the biggest challenges of my life. I had no difficulty solving mathematical problems, but when called upon to give out an answer Mrs. Safran had already checked to be correct, I would remain silent. I still harbored the fear from Haiti that I would be ridiculed for not speaking the language properly.

Mrs. Safran was no fool and she soon figured out what was going on. She was a fairly large, white woman and I have to admit that I was very intimidated by her at the beginning. My entire world had just turned upside down. I was in a new country and forcefully thrown into a different culture I knew absolutely nothing about. My only interaction with white people, in Haiti, involved the few glimpses I caught of them during Saturday night or Sunday morning mass at church in Thomassin. Our priest, Pere Martin, was the closest I ever came to a white person when he would place the communion wafer on my tongue.

Being the great teacher she absolutely was, Mrs. Safran understood and saw through my fears. She began tutoring me during lunch hours. She must have sensed my initial discomfort toward her because she did everything possible to show me warmth and affection. She became a real person to me when she brought in pictures of her family to show me and asked that I do the same.

During our tutoring sessions, Mrs. Safran would make hand gestures or resort to drawing pictures on the board when I just could not grasp the meaning she was trying to convey. She would exaggerate the movements of her mouth, the curvature of her lips and the position of her tongue and teeth to teach me pronunciation skills.

Slowly, I began to trust Mrs. Safran and that trust resulted in my participating more and more in class. One time she asked me to read a passage out loud and I mispronounced the word "child". A few students laughed and for a brief moment, I was right back in that classroom in Haiti feeling just as shameful as I did then. But I quickly recovered when I remembered what Mrs. Safran had told me just a few days before about making mistakes. She said no one was perfect and that remaining silent in class did not prove to anyone that I was any smarter than they thought I was—it only showed that I did not have the guts to try. She pointed out all the foreign students in our class who always spoke freely without fear. So that day when I read out loud and made a mistake and a few students laughed, I mustered up all the courage in the world, and I too laughed. That simple act became my triumph. When Mrs. Safran later on assigned an oral presentation and I made mine in the thickest Haitian accent imaginable, I was more concerned about the content of my work rather than the French-Creole coated delivery.

I learned a very important lesson in the sixth grade that stayed with me well into adulthood. When I took Mrs. Safran's advice and dared to step out and try, some students laughed but there were others who corrected me. As time passed, my mispronunciation of words became less and less funny and many of my initial critics became my greatest mentors. By trying, I gave them an opportunity to help elevate me to a new height.

The Haitian mentality and its response to a call of action, is one that is greatly dependent on the acceptance of people in general. We are afraid of what people say and think about us. We dread being ridiculed and we fall because we are not always able to find a working space between those who accept us and those who criticize us.

There always seem to be more against us than with us. The evil tongues of critics have caused many people to remain inactive.

The Bible especially comments of the effect of an evil tongue in James 3: "*Likewise the tongue is a small part of the body, but it makes great boasts. Consider that a great forest is set on fire by a small spark. The tongue also is a fire, a world of evil among the parts of the body. It corrupts the whole person, sets the whole course of his life on fire and is itself set on fire by hell. All kinds of animals, birds, reptiles and creatures of the sea are being tamed and have been tamed by man, but no man can tame the tongue. It is a restless evil, full of deadly poison.*"

Part of being successful and of not being afraid to step out is one's ability to first expect the evil tongue and second to deal with it—even if that means ignoring it. Once you expect something to happen, you learn to prepare your response to it. In my short professional life, I have attempted many endeavors. Some have worked, more have not. In either case, the evil tongue was always present. I admit that I did not always have a model response, but in retrospect, I believe I would have prevented myself many headaches if I had just anticipated the evil tongue.

The work of changing the face of Haiti is one that is so well worth the effort. Yet, it cannot be expected to be easy and the heroes who dare to spring into action cannot waste time on the few who will demean and point fingers. In Haiti, I diverted all of my attention to the few students who laughed at me in class and was rendered paralyzed by it. In New York, I realized that I could laugh along with them while maintaining my agenda. I realized that when I rose above the feelings of shame and helplessness, my most outspoken critics, ironically became my teachers and greatest supporters.

Thomas Szasz says: "*If you go in search of honey, you must expect to encounter bees.*" Those bees will show up when we decide to invest in our country. We should expect them when, in spite of our financial or educational limitations, we dare to step forward to make a difference.

It takes a lot of character to fight those bees. It takes someone with a strong sense of dedication, determination, and persistence to remain steadfast while dodging stinging bites. It takes a lot of resolve to battle and deny the egotistical self in the pursuit of one's purpose in life. It takes someone who is friend to both patience and humility. It takes someone who understands courage.

People will always talk. Even some we call friends may change their opinions of us at any given time. For that reason, those of us who desire to move forward should never allow people to be our main source of motivation. If we want our country to stop falling, our driving force should always be internally derived. With people, criticism will never be scarce but, paraphrasing the words of Ralph Waldo Emerson, we should take heart in knowing that the reward of a thing well done is simply to have done it. It is not always necessarily in its outcome or in the verbal affirmation of folks. Consider the wisdom of Theodore Roosevelt:

"It is not the critic who counts; the man who points out how the strong man stumbles or where the doer of deeds could have done them better. The credit belongs to the man who is actually in the arena, whose face is marred by dust and sweat and blood; who strives valiantly; who errs and comes up short again and again, because there is not effort without error and shortcoming; but who does actually strive to do the deeds; who knows the great enthusiasms, the great devotions; who spends himself in a worthy cause; who at the best knows in the end the triumph of high achievement, and who at the worst, if he fails at least fails while daring greatly, so that his place shall never be with those cold and timid souls who know neither victory nor defeat."

PART TWO

Rising

7

From the Ashes

Life is many things. It is a bittersweet roller coaster, one minute elevating us to the greatest of heights and the next, plunging us to the deepest of abysses. All the metaphoric descriptions of life I can think of basically culminate into one fact: Life is a challenge.

Life is a challenge Haitians in particular, face with great difficulty. Regardless of the preparation we may have received as children from parents and mentors, we find that we can barely keep our stance when life makes a sudden turn. We have trouble withstanding the obstacles of life and sometimes, it is difficult not to conclude that we have been singled out to suffer.

As we find ourselves in solitude, in desperation, amid ashes and debris, amid the shattered stones of what was once our mighty fortress, we wonder if we will ever have the strength, the energy, the courage, or the nerves to even make an attempt at rising. Would it not be easier to just remain here in our dungeon, where life is a matter of routine incidence rather than a challenge we eagerly face?

Here at the bottom, occasional flashes of sanity and memories of a dignified existence periodically compete for the spotlight, but lose the battle every time to a more powerful present reality. Here where we are, the voice of pure conscience is loud and clear—there is no room for disconnected intellectualism and rationalization. At the bottom of the abyss, we are forced to accept a new existence. We are forced to create a new normal.

There is something very spiritually humbling about being in the ashes. We find very few friends and even fewer words of comfort. In the ashes, negative labels create even deeper psychological scars. The ashes have a way of eliminating all external boosting forces. There are few true supporters and fanatics to cheer us onward.

The condition of being in the ashes forces one to assess and appreciate the raw realities of life. In the ashes there is no sustainable pretense. There is no covering up, no masquerading of the true self. All material camouflage has been eliminated and we lie naked not only to the self but to the entire world. Every flaw, every discrepancy, every lie and every truth is openly revealed.

Being in the ashes can be good because there are many important lessons there to be learned. However, as Haitians, the ashes have been our reality for so long that many of us are starting to accept this condition of suffering as normal. Today we are at a crucial point and a very important decision has to be made. Do we lie here and die or do we rise? Do we gather those shattered stones and use them as foundation for something stronger or do we remain passive, uncomfortably at ease amid the remnants of what we once were?

A parade of cheering voices we do not have. Our rising, therefore, has to be a direct manifestation of our own inner strength. We can empower ourselves only by drawing on something from the inside—by relying primarily on ourselves.

To be successful, we must use the ashes as a learning experience—as a way of taking a real hard look at ourselves and realizing what we truly are about. We need to search for viable pieces among the debris that have retained memory of our past achievements. Whether they are people or inanimate objects, they hold the essence of who we really are. They remember every one of our triumphs.

I borrow from Ecclesiastes in the Bible to say that there really is nothing new under the sun. Every road that leads to every torment or every victory has already been traveled by people before us. The idea is for us to not feel special in neither triumph nor failure. Instead, we should learn from people in our past who suffered the same atrocities. We should study their exit strategies and modify and perfect every move to fit our own situation.

Rising from the ashes is not a singular, abrupt move that culminates into sudden triumph. Rather, it starts as an irrevocable decision to make a crucial first move in the positive direction. This means having a reason to want to make the move in the first place. To rise from the ashes, we must first make mental adjustments. This involves a change in our attitude toward all that is positive. When we make that change, we cease to blame others for our situation, we cease denying the fact that we do need help and we cease to be content in our present state of passive living.

Successful people learn to search the debris for remnants of allies they once had, and more importantly, they search the debris and assess for points of weakness. As the black box provides significant information after a plane crashes, within our mess are many of the clues needed to figure out where we went wrong. We only need to search honestly and make a decision to learn from the experience.

When a house collapses, the debris is proof that the house was on shaky ground to begin with. Supporting forces thought to be adequate turned out to not be the case, but that does not mean the house cannot be erected again. On the contrary, this new knowledge enables the successful builder to now create a much stronger, resilient and firm edifice.

The lessons learned while being in the ashes give rise to opportunities that otherwise would have gone un-seized. The ashes enable us to get out of the egotistical realm and allow shared past experiences, present opportunities and a vast array of other variables to catapult us back into action.

Rising from the ashes means we cannot be afraid to face the world. As we lie there in shame and exhaustion, we cannot forget that the world is looking at us. Some people are hoping we never get up because it is only in our failure that they can themselves triumph. Some are rooting for us to rise because in our ascent lies their own salvation. Most importantly, some are learning about the world and themselves through our experience. They are the silent observers whose characters and destinations we will impact greatly as they study our every move. Our children are being shaped every day by either our action or our lack of it. As we lie silent in the ashes, we must remember that we are still loudly dictating to our youth the ways in which they should respond to life as a challenge.

If we are honest with ourselves, we should begin to realize that even in the ashes we cannot afford to give up.

We cannot afford to miss the opportunities that are all around us. We have to gather from the ashes all usable pieces of our previous life and patch them together to start rebuilding.

We can be successful even in our present condition. Success is being able to use whatever life throws our way, whatever is in our present situation to make a connection with where we want to end up. So when life crumbles all around us and we feel marked and persecuted, we should not despair. When the amazing history of Haiti seems to not matter and when it seems like the world is laughing at us, we should take heart. We cannot perish unless we allow ourselves to. We only need to become creative at finding avenues of escape. When we decide to rise from the ashes, we'll become stronger, smarter and we'll gain wisdom with every challenge.

8

The Right Attitude as the Ball Rolls

Although a cliché, I love the roller coaster description of life. As a young child I marveled at the analogy, imagining the thrilling experience life was going to become for me. I could not wait to grow up in order to fully enjoy my gift.

There is no question that the old saying definitely has its merit. I remember my grandmother stating all the time in her native Creole: "*La vi ya se yon boule kap woule*

(Life is a rolling ball)." She used to always tell me: *"Sometimes you'll find yourself on top but you will also have your share of the bottom side."*

As a young girl, all I cared about was the thrill of a roller coaster ride and I could not appreciate the metaphoric value of my grandmother's warning. As I grew older however, I began to use the bits of information my grandmother provided in formulating my own concept of life. I began to fully understand the meaning of her words. Maturity and experience allowed me to appreciate the idea of the "bottom side" and the years gave me clarity and understanding.

There are two very important lessons I learned from my grandmother's teachings. The first lesson relates to the implied concept of change. The human experience, from birth until death, is characterized by constant changes in appearance, thought processes, beliefs, etc…The roller coaster itself is characterized by changes in velocity, changes in position and oftentimes changes in direction.

From a scientific perspective, even if we choose to remain at rest, it is a difficult task to accomplish. The fact that we are alive makes it impossible for us to not participate in change. When we breathe, when we move, every time our hearts beat, we are changing.

We take part in change even when we are not aware of it—or perhaps choose to ignore it. For example, whether we want to acknowledge it or not, the change of government officials where we live affects our lives. Changes in Haiti affect our lives. Many of us reminisce about the old days when we could vacation or live there in peace. Many of us have uprooted our families and left for places much less conducive to our needs, in exchange for a little security. Change, in the negative direction, has chased many of us away from a land we truly love.

The older I get, the more I realize the roller coaster is not all fun and games—not every shift in direction is welcoming, not every movement is eagerly anticipated. Yet, if we choose to liken life to a roller coaster, we must accept the fact that change has to occur. We must learn proper methods of dealing with that change. Our actions sometimes indicate that we only expect and pray for change when things are not well. Whether on top of the world or crushed beneath its weight, we have to anticipate change.

Whenever we fail to appreciate the concept of change, we allow decisions to be made for us without our consent or awareness. We allow people who do not share our values to speak and act on our behalf. We sit quietly and watch other people take care of our precious business. We end up developing an attitude of indifference rather than success.

The fear of dealing with change keeps us from being innovative. Nothing new and exciting ever comes from performing a task the same exact way every time. However, a very slight change in movement, thought, or perception, can result in unbelievable new creations that otherwise would have never been realized. Stagnation accomplishes very little but the more we move, the more we act, and the more we act, the more opportunities and possibilities we create. As we become creators of opportunities, we have no choice but to develop an attitude that is strong and healthy.

The second important lesson I learned from my grandmother's statement is that life is a gift. We make our big entrance into it completely clueless. Our exit is perhaps no different. In between the two, however, we can pack in lifetimes of adventure, of exploration, of learning. With God's perfect creation as our stage, we have at our disposal all the tools necessary to create the most awesome of productions. Life gives us the freedom to be creative and to have wonderful experiences. It is a gift we can infect others with. We can use it as a torch that brings joy, hope and satisfaction to so many people in need.

Many of us fail to use our gift properly. We often take our lives for granted. We carry out our daily chores and actually believe we are in control, when in fact, we have surrendered our lives to other people—or other things. We take this wonderful gift of life and toss it away. We become very busy fulfilling the desires of others, realizing the agendas of others and living a life that is entirely not our own. We lose perspective, we lose sight and we become lost to ourselves. We forget that we have a purpose and destiny to fulfill.

When we fail to recognize the importance of our gift, we get stuck into what I call *passive living*. Passive living is performing routines that in the end do not contribute to anything progressive. It is the failure to properly use the life that has been given to us. Being satisfied in a present limited state and failing to advance is living passively. Never taking time to help another person or to put someone else's needs ahead of one's own is living passively. Watching opportunities pass by and waiting for good fortune to fall from the sky is living passively. Not making a difference, not taking action, believing that we cannot be more than we are, are all examples of passive living.

We were not created to just exist and when we live passively, we waste the greater portion of the natural resources we were born with. We should be active participants in this world, if not for our sake, definitely for that of our children. We should place ourselves in positions where we can squeeze out the very essence of life, feed from it and bless others with it as well.

Life is a school that teaches about unexplored places and deep regions of our souls. Life is an adventure. We never know what to expect next. The more we live the more we encounter. The more we encounter the more we learn. The more we learn the more we want to live and the more we realize that a lifetime is actually quite short. To make our contribution, we actually have to seize every opportunity and become very proficient in managing our time.

Life is a gift we receive, but fulfilling our purpose here is our gift back to the world. When we rise to action, not for the wrong reasons, but simply because it is the right thing to do, we are using our gift properly. We can use our gift by feeding, nurturing, loving, comforting, elevating. When we decide to rise up and give of our time with no ulterior motive, we begin to fulfill our destiny. We begin to become a part of something greater than ourselves that in turn will complete our purpose.

In my grandmother's roller coaster description of life, there are two crucial points that can make or break even the very best of plans. At the top where we soar, we should be careful to rejoice but never to gloat. We have a responsibility to remain very focused and diligent instead of allowing arrogance and conceit to have their way. As a goal is reached, we cannot afford to become idle. There is a passage in the book of Proverbs that addresses this very issue. The New International Version translates Ch. 24: 30-34 as follows: "*I went past the field of the sluggard, past the vineyard of the man who lacks judgment; thorns had come up everywhere, the ground was covered with weeds, and the stone wall was in ruins. I applied my heart to what I observed and learned a lesson from what I saw; a little sleep, a little slumber, a little folding of the hands to rest— and poverty will come on you like a bandit and scarcity like an armed man.*"

When our ride hits bottom, we reach another crucial point. Unless we remain focused, we may allow ourselves to be crushed, never to rise again. This position is even more important than the previous. Here, we have to seize every opportunity and use positive energy to muscle us back up into successful territory.

If we understand and accept life to be a roller

coaster and we have the right attitude, the periods of achievement will not render us arrogant and the periods of failure will not render us hopeless. They will be milestones that will enable us to continuously adjust our course in order to keep the ride moving smoothly.

I believe the second we come into this world, God has already armed us with everything we need to develop into the people He created us to be. The saddest impact on our legacy is to be lucky enough to have experienced life at this point in time, and to have missed the point of it all. We should be part of the working movement that helps others because it is the only way we can begin to determine our purpose and rightly fulfill it.

I believe our attitude should reflect a sense of gratitude for the precious gift of life. The way we carry ourselves, the way we react to situations and the way we perceive the world all factor in. We must take care to not allow the down times on the roller coaster to determine our attitude.

Regardless of the situation we find ourselves in, we should always strive for a positive outlook. When we approach life with a positive attitude we can pinpoint our success with precision. We can anticipate the degree of success we can achieve based on an attitude that is backed by preparation.

A positive attitude always leads to success regardless of outcome. For instance, Mohammed Ali always had a great attitude before every fight. Aspiring politicians campaign with the most positive of attitudes until the very end. However, we all know that Mohammed Ali was not always happy with every single fight. We know not every politician wins every campaign. A positive attitude does not completely eliminate the possibility of coming up short. Though it increases the likelihood of victory, a good attitude will not always guarantee a desired outcome.

I did not use the word *success* in the last sentence for a simple reason. Though we often associate success with the attainment of a particular goal, many times, success is really obtained in the *process* of completing the task. In the next chapter I explore this in greater detail, but for now it is important to realize that preparation plus a great attitude ensure success regardless of the outcome of any situation. Mohammed Ali was successful before even setting foot in a boxing ring because his attitude was that of a successful fighter. A successful individual has an attitude that exudes self-confidence and allows focus on matters that are truly important.

Some people are particularly good at displaying a positive attitude. I cannot count the number of times I have called someone crazy for wanting to jump out of an airplane or for getting back on a motorcycle or a race car after a life-threatening accident involving those very same vehicles. It is a positive attitude that makes them want to get back to business until the desired outcome is obtained.

As young Haitians thrust into the American culture, many of us have encountered problems concerning the self and attitude. Oftentimes it is difficult to feel as equally important as everyone else. We face so many barriers that sometimes it becomes impossible for us to accurately evaluate our worth. We are constantly striving to prove ourselves as we learn, as we work, even as we play. We often forget who we are as we measure ourselves against the backdrop of American culture. This distraction, this lack of focus, has a huge negative impact on our attitude.

The following statements reveal an ugly truth about our attitude as a people:

> *Haitien pa gin tet ansam.*
> *Haitians can't get along with one another.*
>
> *Haitien pa fe anyin ki serie.*
> *Haitians are not serious about anything.*
>
> *Fo se pa haitien pou ou ta ye!*
> *You could not be anything else but Haitian!*

Haitien toujou konin.
Haitians always pretend to know.

Haitien pa jam gin chance.
Haitians are never lucky.

Haitien se bet ki pi Ingra.
Haitians are the most ungrateful of animals.

Haitien pa vle we ou gin anyin.
Haitians begrudge each other their possessions.

Haitien se pep ki pi modi.
Haitians are the most cursed of all people.

We routinely repeat many statements such as those without even thinking. Yet, all of those negative sayings are really applicable to people in general regardless of nationality. The fact that we attach the Haitian label to them is gratuitous self-condemnation. Those faults, as we come across them, are common to humans in general and not only Haitians. When we fail to realize that fact, we give other people priority status over our own. When we have an issue with a Korean or Cuban merchant, we do not demean their entire race and yet if we have a spat with a Haitian business owner, we swear not to ever again patronize Haitian-owned businesses.

Our attitude toward our own people has to change. We have to deprogram our minds and get rid of all the negative sentiments we have accumulated. We need to remember that first we are humans with imperfections and second we are Haitians. We do things to hurt each other because we are humans and not because we are Haitians. As Haitians, we are different from people of other nations, but as human beings we are all the same. Not as Haitians, but as humans, we are capable of love. Not as Haitians, but as humans, we are also capable of treachery.

We can begin to create an attitude for success no matter where we find ourselves on the rolling ball, when we support each other and decide to stop being our own worst enemy.

9

Success

Everyone wants to be successful. Students, parents, entrepreneurs, politicians, religious leaders etc... We all want to successfully accomplish all tasks we undertake and we want to be fully compensated for our hard work. There is absolutely nothing wrong with desiring success as long as we do not only associate it with dollar bills and fame.

Success is neither a condition nor an achieved level

of stability. Rather, I believe it is a *continuous attempt* to accomplish calculated objectives necessary to achieve a particular goal, realize a particular dream or satisfy a particular need. This definition of success implies a state of constant motion—a progressive movement toward an aim.

Success is always making adjustments to enable or facilitate the happening of a "thing" we want very badly. It is not the attainment of the "thing" itself, but it is in the actual process we go through in order to get it. It is in the sweat that we put out, the long hours we put in and it is in the decision we make to remain steadfast. It is in the lessons we learn as we strive to constantly reach higher levels. This is the reason we can make bold statements about our success even in the absence of tangible evidence. We become able to visualize ourselves as successful regardless of the position we may temporarily find ourselves in.

Understanding the true definition of success sheds

light on the widely held misconception that successful people are greedy. Many wonderful individuals have gained notoriety simply because they are not understood. Critics do not understand why they move from one project to another, always attempt to better themselves, or continue to take calculated risks.

Too many of us fail to understand that although true success often results in material possessions, those items themselves are not success. They are merely wonderful by-products of well-executed plans or strategies. Often, the actual realization of a goal is not the driving force behind the actions of a successful individual. For this reason, a man with a hefty bank account will still wake up early in the morning to go to work and will still continue to go to school to stretch his mind.

To remain steadfast on a successful path, we must begin with a desire to succeed—a flaming, unwavering longing to gather all ammunition, use wisely all resources, and test the limits of all possibilities. To desire strongly is to want with a powerful and insatiable hunger that accepts no defeat, no compromise, and no substitution. A strong desire helps us build the potential to create success. When we have that yearning, we do not give way, we do not give up, and we do not give in to any temptation that would make us lose focus. Our desire makes us stand our ground and critics sooner or later realize they can neither stop nor deter us.

We can become successful individuals all working toward the common goal of building a better Haiti. However, to be truly effective, we must understand that success requires endurance. We have to be able to withstand, resist, tolerate and even suffer sometimes.

To ensure we endure, we must not allow emotions to be our prime motivator. We must refrain from making emotional decisions because as soon as the emotions subside, so will our desire to help. For example, the person who attempts to lose weight solely to satisfy a significant other, finds that motivation is easily lost once that particular other is no longer that significant. The temporary sentiment tied to that person was the driving force rather than healthy, good living.

The same principle holds true for our decisions as they relate to Haiti. If our attempt to help is only motivated by emotions, we will begin but we will not be able to sustain. Many people begin to contribute to great Haitian organizations only to stop the moment they receive unfavorable news about the country.

Our success is directly dependent on our ability to endure. This means that long after the emotional speeches are done, long after the event that caused the emotion that caused the action is forgotten, long after we've watched leader after leader drop off, and long after the act of helping has ceased to satisfy a selfish motive, we will still continue to push onward. We will persist because our vision for a greater country is much stronger than any temporary reaction our emotions could have caused.

To put one's hands in the pot of helping Haiti is to have persistence. Persistence is faith, desire, and determination wrapped in one. Persistence builds character and strength and it promotes creativity. It forces one to think beyond the limits of his or her mind. Because of persistence, failures are not devastating but become reasons to perhaps change direction. A burning desire fuels our faith in ourselves, and persistence always leads to success.

When we are successful, we create our own opportunities and life becomes a wonderful experience of challenges encountered and conquered.

10

Taking the First Step toward Success

America is the ultimate melting pot of talent, of culture, of everything that is different quilted into one. It is the amalgamation of myriads of independently working parts, each performing well defined and specific functions crucial to the maintenance and advancement of the nation.

This variety creates opportunities that are limitless in nature.

A Chinese philosopher once wrote: *"The journey of a thousand miles begins with a single step."* America did not become the power it is today overnight. By the same token, we cannot expect to have Haiti turn around in a few short years.

We have to learn to take a first step but very few are in a position to do that. Many people are just not ready because first, they have to make certain adjustments in their general attitude to prepare themselves to move. For example, many Haitians readily accept poverty as a virtue. Because they are afraid to fail, they wear a cloak of indifference as a prize and condition themselves to find comfort in discomfort itself. Even when they know they can do better, even when information is readily available, they make an active choice to remain stagnant. They fight to remain in a mechanical, robotic mode even when all arrows point to a need for change. They allow negative factors to overpower and freeze them.

Taking our first step is easy if we realize that success does not just happen. Like most things in life that are dear, it comes with a price. As a people, we often are not willing to pay the price of educating ourselves on relevant issues. We are not willing to pay the price of adjusting our attitude in order to become more receptive to ideas and more assertive in our behavior. We are not willing to pay the price of rising above racism and discrimination and boldly taking possession of what is justly ours. Finally, we are not willing to pay the price of failing. Our unwillingness to take initiative enslaves our spirit and locks up our sense of creativity.

The price of educating ourselves involves the recognition and exploration of opportunities as they come along. For example, we can discipline ourselves to listen to radio programs that address matters relevant to our purpose. We can trade trashy television programs for others that offer excellent useful information on diverse subjects. We can replace idleness with time spent on the internet or at the library. Many people falsely believe that college is the only place one can obtain a valid education. In this day of technological marvel, it is easy for us to read and research ourselves into remarkable experts.

The price of adjusting our attitude involves utilizing to a greater extent, the art of listening—the practice of making every attempt to fully understand another before formulating our own argument. It involves the willingness to open ourselves to new experiences. Above all, improving our attitude requires that we hold ourselves to a higher esteem and truly believe that we can make a difference and be more than we are right now.

The price of rising above racism and discrimination involves making an irrevocable decision to keep knocking until doors open, to stop blaming a system for our failures, to build up strength and power by promoting unity, and to create our very own opportunities.

The price of risk taking involves the willingness, patience and faith to believe in the unknown and anticipate positive outcomes. That, I know, is easier said than done. When I face challenges pertaining to risk taking and failure, a wonderful phrase I hear often always comes to mind: *"A setback is a setup for a comeback."* I also believe to fail is to succeed. Failing implies attempt and continuous attempt is success. When we attempt, we seek and when we seek, we always gain knowledge and wisdom that serve us in future attempts.

My hope is that as Haitians, we will each feel an urge to take a first step. Whether it involves our personal lives or the life of our country, we need to move forward toward a future that is more promising.

With every step, we will begin to prepare ourselves to receive greater blessings. A nineteenth century writer once wrote: *"Unless a man has trained himself for his chance, the chance will only make him look ridiculous. A great occasion is worth to a man exactly what his preparation enables him to make of it."*

We need to prepare ourselves by beginning to pay the price for the rewards that await us individually and as a people. In the words of Dennis Kimbro and Napoleon Hill): *"Opportunities abound. The world waits to judge our valuation of ourselves, to see what we do with those opportunities that have escaped our grasp for so many years. The door has now opened, and the freedom to walk through is ours."*

11

We Don't Have to be Big to do Big Things!

"If you think you are too small to do big things, try doing small things in a big way!" I love that statement because of its emphasis on the importance of small acts. I saw a little girl recently on television. Her name was Alex and she was eight years old. Alex was diagnosed with

cancer when she was a baby. As soon as she could communicate her wishes to her parents, Alex used a phrase she undoubtedly heard grown ups utter a million times: *"When life throws you lemons, make lemonade!"*

Alex took the phrase seriously and started a small lemonade stand in her neighborhood. She donated all the meager proceeds for cancer research. By the time the television program aired, there were no fewer than two hundred of Alex's Lemonade Stands throughout the country. They were all started and run by individuals who loved Alex's idea and felt she was a hero. Perhaps that idea was just the extra push many of them facing the same predicament needed to get started on something meaningful.

Alex's Lemonade Stands have raised and donated more than two hundred thousand dollars, but Alex is not portrayed worldwide as a "big shot." On the contrary, she is a frail, tiny, little girl who dared to think big in spite of her afflictions.

In the context of thinking big, the story of Helen Keller comes to mind. This is a woman who was born in 1880 and at the age of eighteen months became both deaf and blind from meningitis. I imagine that people who came across that little girl generally felt sorry for her—how very small, by any standard, she must have appeared to them all!

Growing up was very difficult for Helen and her family. Communication was virtually impossible until Helen's parents hired a woman by the name of Anne Sullivan to tutor their daughter. This was under the advice of Alexander Graham Bell who was also a teacher of the deaf. Anne was able to develop a method of communication that actually worked for Helen. She made signs in Helen's palms that the student grew to understand and eventually became her brilliant means of communication. Anne went everywhere with Helen, including college, where she would actually translate the lectures into Helen's hands.

Helen Keller eventually learned to speak by pressing her fingers against Anne's throat and imitating the vibrations she felt coming through. She graduated College Cum Laude. She went on to write her autobiography, *The Story of My Life*, and many other books. Helen became an advocate for the blind, and spoke out against child labor and capital punishment. She became world known receiving high honors both at home and abroad. She received an honorary degree from Harvard University and in the year 1964, President Lyndon B. Johnson conferred upon her the United States' highest civilian honor, the Presidential Medal of Freedom. To this day, the work of the little girl who could neither see, nor hear, continues through foundations established to help the handicapped.

We do not have to be big to think big. We do not have to be big to accomplish big things. Every small achievement is not only important but necessary. In an article entitled, *The Importance of Little Things*, Buddy Sheets remarks that successful people treat the nonessentials like what they really are—the essentials. He writes: "...*They have found that little drops of water and little grains of sand make the mighty ocean and the pleasant land.*"

Before becoming known worldwide, Alex was just a little girl battling the devastating effects of cancer. Before Helen Keller was able to graduate from College, she suffered through the agonizing task of learning and processing every small symbol drawn onto her palms. The small things are so essential because they become the foundation upon which big things can stand. Doing small things does not mean we do not have a vision of greatness. It actually means the opposite.

There are many small people among us who do great things. The man in Haiti, without sophisticated equipment, who tends to the land and produces food through back breaking labor, does wonders for the agricultural welfare of the country. The sassy woman with a sharp tongue who sells at the marketplace, though considered ungraceful and void of social etiquette, does wonders for the economic welfare of the country. The poor father whose meager wages from degrading jobs pay his children's tuition, is a huge contributor to the educational and vocational welfare of the country. No person is ever too small to think big and accomplish feats of extraordinary significance.

12

Effective Communication

"It is the mark of an educated mind to be able to entertain a thought without accepting it."--Aristotle

Communication is defined in the Cambridge Advanced Learner's Dictionary as: *"Sharing information with others by speaking, writing, moving your body or using other signals."* Communication can be verbal or non-verbal.

Dialogue is conversation between two or more people. It is communication that is healthy, productive and satisfying. Dialogue should be free flowing in an atmosphere of mutual respect, where all opinions are respected.

Dialogue, as a form of communication, is essential. Studies, however, show that only seven percent of the time what is said is heard, and what is meant is actually understood. At any given time during a conversation, the spoken word is in direct competition with other facets of communication such as body language and tone of voice.

Communication involves sending and receiving messages. The sole purpose of communicating is the successful transmission of ideas and thoughts. Those ideas and thoughts are then filtered through a communication carrier. The carrier allows the listener to sift everything he hears through his own set of biases, values, and experiences. At the end of that process, a message is actually received.

In any given conversation, all things being considered, the meaning of a message conveyed can be completely different from what was intended by the speaker. This does not mean that either the listener or the speaker is at fault. It simply accounts for the fact that each individual has his or her own set of filters that actually modify the spoken word.

In the Haitian community, I find that though we talk, we rarely communicate. We do not engage in dialogue where people actually listen. We do not always create an environment of acceptance, tolerance and openness. We do not concern ourselves with the reactions our words create and we certainly underestimate the effects of body language and tonality of voice. We do not realize, in a conversation, that what we mean to say is actually not as important as the meaning we do transfer. If our listeners become angry, for example, that is the meaning we transferred. That is most important above any other meaning we intended to convey.

As Haitians, we experience communication glitches in every aspect of our lives. Whether we are interacting with family members, friends, or the general public, many of us undervalue the importance of proper dialogue and communication. We talk, but we remain oblivious to the messages we send and receive. We look to assert ourselves and to advocate our positions without allowing others to feel safe and comfortable when they share dissenting opinions. We tend to force our opinions on others and limit opportunities for meaningful discussions. We often communicate in manners that are overly aggressive, hurtful and even abusive.

A meaningful conversation should never be a competition where there are winners and losers. When that form of contest exists, we may cause many listeners to opt for silence, in an effort to disengage themselves from controversy and conflict. Many people prefer to remain silent when they feel threatened in expressing their true thoughts and feelings. This is a major communication block that can only have negative results.

In any given verbal interaction, we have to maintain positive regard for others and treat them as valuable contributors. Even when we disagree with folks, we are still obligated to respect their opinions. We have to be mindful of their backgrounds and experiences as factors that greatly determine their stand. We have a responsibility to not always be defensive but to realize that solutions to big problems are the collective result of different ideas integrated, facts examined, arguments considered, and several points of view combined.

For dialogue to be effective, we also have to practice well the art of listening. We should listen not only to hear, but also to seek understanding. We should always ask for clarification when necessary because it is very important to understand clearly the other person's logic. It is very possible for two people to engage in verbal exchange for a long period of time without really communicating—that is without transmitting the messages they really set out to.

Often, our communication problems also stem from an inability to differentiate between what we know and what we believe. In his book, *Wisdom of the Ages*, Wayne Dyer makes a vivid distinction between *believing* and *knowing*. He describes *belief* as something we acquire from other people's experiences. *Knowing*, on the other hand, is the opposite because we come to know things from our own encounters.

As Haitians, we confuse the two quite often. We believe in things we've never experienced and yet we strongly profess to know them. For instance, when I examine my value system, I realize that many things that shape my thoughts are based on beliefs that have been passed down to me. Many things I think I know, I only really just believe.

Sometime ago, I read an old story about a very holy man. He was so righteous that God came to him one day and said: "*You may ask one question, and I will personally answer it.*" The holy man, knowing that he had just been given a big responsibility, answered: "*Would you mind giving me a little time to decide on the right question?*" God responded: "*When you have the question, I will be here.*"

The holy man thought and thought. He knew that this was a very unusual opportunity—to get an answer to a question directly from God. He thought about all the things people were curious about. He wanted to make sure he asked the one question that most people would want answered. Finally, he decided that the most popular question would be: "What happens after death?"

When God came to him, the holy man said: "*I want*

to know what happens after we die." God replied, *"You got it"*, and the holy man dropped dead. You only really know something after you have experienced it yourself.

When I first read that passage from an internet website, I could not help contrasting it to behavior I have witnessed many times in my life—heated political discussions dangerously bordering on insult; mounting emotions giving way to abrupt physical gestures; and unwarranted personal attacks when all else fails. Those are all expressive behaviors meant to confirm knowledge that, often, are merely acquired beliefs.

Pretending to have all the answers is one of our biggest flaws as Haitians. It is difficult sometimes for us to admit we simply do not know. A friend once told me a story about a doctor who became furious when a contractor attempted to enlighten him on some basic concepts of construction. It did not take the good doctor long to announce that he was no idiot and that he held a medical degree. It took the doctor no time to inform the contractor of his social position relative to that of a physician.

When we think we know it all, we cannot communicate effectively. Every conversational encounter becomes a platform for us to display our eloquence, our pride and our righteousness. We seek to dominate and the encounter cannot bear any fruit. As a result, we end up with shouting matches and real communication is hindered.

Another factor at the core of our communication problems involves the concept of paradigms. In a book written by Stephen Covey, *The Seven Habits of Highly Effective People*, the author describes the concept of paradigms as being our perception, or simply as the way we see and interpret things.

The way we see the world has a lot to do with our value system. The way we interpret things has a lot to do with our experiences, our cultural beliefs, our moral character etc… Unless we are able to perform what Covey refers to as a *"paradigm shift,"* it will always be difficult to relate effectively with one another. A paradigm shift allows an individual to see other people's points of view through their lenses rather than his own.

There are many instances where an accident occurs and every eyewitness renders a different account of the event to the police. Sometimes they are all correct. Our world is not of one dimension and as such, we have to make allowances for perceptions and points of view that are different from our own. We have to accept the possibility that more exists outside of our own perceptions. There are physical, mental, and emotional regions that are unknown to us simply because our individual value systems may not allow us to explore those areas.

The idea of paradigms and perception is made powerful in the following example borrowed from Joanne A. in *The Power of Paradigms*. Imagine yourself sitting at a square table with three other individuals. In the middle of the table you clearly see the letter "*M*" printed. Note that if you ask each of the other three people what they see on the center of the table, they may each have a different answer. The one to your left could possibly see an *E*, the one directly across from you could say *W* and the one to your right could possibly see the number *3*. This explains why several eyewitnesses can have different accounts of the same event.

This simple example sheds great light on an important fact: A person's perception dictates how he sees the world and how he reacts to events and other people. Sometimes, it is important for us to step outside of our world, if only temporarily, in an attempt to gain understanding.

If during a conversation, we really attempt to value each other's contribution, there would be no room for disastrous outcomes. In the table example, all four individuals can swear to death that they are correct in their interpretation. They can become very aggressive in defending their positions and at the end they will all remain with the same opinions. But look what happens when one person, instead of remaining rigid to his own perception, allows himself to shift paradigms and switches seats with another. All of a sudden, he sees and experiences a brand new event and he realizes that not all truths may be absolute. He is able to see an entire world that exists beyond his own, and with that comes brand new thoughts, brand new ideas, brand new opportunities, brand new possibilities, and brand new solutions.

In order for us to begin to make many of the changes that are necessary for our country, we have to improve our communication skills. We have to be able to not bruise as easily those who share opinions other than our own. We have to be able to step out of our world, and see someone else's point of view. We have to not allow ourselves to engage in counteractive behavior and resort to personal verbal attacks when we are cornered. The words

of Evelyn Beatrice Hall are very powerful: *"I may*

disapprove of what you say, but I will defend to the death

your right to say it."

13

Into the Eyes of our Monsters

Many of us have a natural tendency to want to detach ourselves from controversy or conflict. When things go wrong we sometimes want to run away instead of facing the problems head on. We forget that action taken early saves both time and energy.

It is a defense mechanism to keep from the forefront of our minds all things that make us feel uncomfortable.

Haiti is such a thing. We often stash all things related to her way back in the dark crevices of our minds along with other bothersome issues of our lives. We make the decision to move on with our lives and ignore what we know to be important.

Our hidden dilemmas, however, do not always remain in the dark forever. Every now and then they may begin to surface. Like children competing for the attention of a parent, they often become more and more pressing— more and more urgent.

The human mind, on the other hand, is wonderfully creative. To keep the nagging pests in place, it cleverly enables certain monsters to come into existence. The fear monster scares us into believing that if we respond to the pressure, danger may result. The rejection monster tells us that our actions would never be accepted anyway because we simply are not good enough. The procrastination monster tells us to focus on other things today because we will always have tomorrow to deal with the urgency. Little by little, more monsters are created and they begin to gain control over us. The more that happens, the less likely we are to respond to our call. Being overwhelmed, but really feeling justified, we end up bailing out.

There are some, however, who learn to stare straight into the eyes of their monsters. They realize that doing so is very empowering in every single area of their lives. They stare any monster in the eye initially to measure it up. That is the only way to size it up and find out what it is all about. Often, what we perceive to be monsters are actually little nagging pests that just need to be dealt with. We cannot, in all our wisdom, create a successful strategy to deal with life's problems unless we have a very clear idea of all that they entail. We cannot prepare ourselves to deal with something we do not fully understand.

We stare our monsters in the eyes every time we ask questions; every time we slow down to listen and observe;

and every time we humble ourselves enough to learn all facts prior to making a final decision or accusation.

It is important to bring Haiti to the forefront. It is vital, at this point in time, to give her top priority. Whatever personal situations we may find ourselves in, we must be strong and decisive enough to stand up to every monster. Like a fighter before a match, we have to square off the shoulders and stand face to face locking eyes with our opponent.

Every time we fail to stare our monsters in the eyes we make a decision to remain inactive and we never get to face the problems they hide so well. If we never face and evaluate our problems, how do we know that they have us licked? When we refuse to stare into the eyes of our monsters, we are an incompetent army waiving tired white flags without knowing if war had ever been declared.

14

Our Children

It is a logical assumption to make that whatever work we accomplish today may not necessarily bear fruit in our lifetime. We may be lucky enough to witness gradual changes, but the realization of our ultimate goal, as it relates to Haiti, is many years ahead of us. As such, we cannot underestimate the importance of our children.

Far from the context of Haiti, every reasonable

parent understands the responsibility that comes with children. Regardless of social class or personalities, children allow parents to become a little less selfish, a little more understanding and a whole lot more generous.

To be successful with our children in the present and to ensure their success in the future, we must become more than mere guardians or providers of basic needs. As we do for the physical, we have to pay careful attention to the mental and psychological health of our children. We must allow them room for individuality, freedom for self-expression, and we have to show interest in the things that are most important to them. While perhaps all Haitian parents are excellent at providing basic necessities, we often neglect the emotional and psychological components of a child's makeup.

Our children are little adults. The clumsiness of a child and the physical manifestations of a work in progress hide many truths. Children are nothing less than complete individuals with the same desire to be understood as adults, with the same eagerness to be successful as adults and with the same feelings of disappointment that adults experience. They have the same need to be encouraged, validated and appreciated.

I remember growing up in a culture where a child dared not stare into the eyes of an adult and phrases like *"ti moun pa gin volonte (children have no will)"* were constant reminders that I was considered to be less than a whole person. The same person today who makes decisions about occupational contracts and family issues is the same thirty years ago who made decisions involving crayon color and doll preference. My drawings as a five year-old were as important to me then as my contracts are today. My need for validation was as great then as it is now.

I hope to not be misunderstood. Whatever positive attributes I have today are greatly due to my culture and the wonderful people who guided me. My grandmother's love lashes at the age of six taught me that taking somebody else's property was inexcusable and since taking her penny that day without permission, I have never stolen another thing. To this day, respecting my elders is of utmost importance. My culture lavished me with priceless values but it also created certain attitudes that, as an adult, I had to learn to suppress. It took me years to overcome timidity and reap the benefits of being assertive. Sometimes our best intentions, as parents, do not necessarily create the best results.

It is very important for parents to fully understand the fundamental needs of children. The first and most important of those is a child's desire to always feel loved. In *Relational Parenting*, Dr. Ross Campbell expresses the following truth: *"To consistently express love for the child is the basis of effective parenting. The basic needs of children do not change, and the first of those needs is to feel loved."*

Most parents feel that their children are always aware of their love. Nothing could be further from the truth, especially in the Haitian household. Research shows over and over again that children are not always aware of the degree to which their parents love them.

We need to consistently tell and show our children we love them especially when disciplinary actions on our part may confuse them. Children may not be aware that love will not allow them to stay out late, but they are certain that love is a hug or a word of understanding after a harsh denial. They may sometimes forget that love provides shelter and food, but they always remember love when a parent willingly spends time with them. They are certain that love is a parent's active participation in the things that interest them.

Children demand and deserve unconditional love. This is love that is given freely regardless of who the child is, regardless of how tall, how short, how fat, how thin the child is, and regardless of the way the child acts. Unconditional love tells a child that he will be nurtured and that his feelings and needs will always be considered.

Unconditional love does not spoil a child. It does not send the wrong signal. A parent is well able to discipline a child while providing unconditional love. Unconditional love does not mean that if Marsha disrespects a teacher in school, she comes home to a loving mother who tells her she's the greatest and loves her no matter what. What it does mean, is that Marsha would come home to a parent who would find out the facts and take all necessary corrective actions. Throughout the entire process, however, the parent would make sure that the child receives a very important message—the behavior may be unacceptable but Marsha, herself, is an acceptable human being who made a mistake. Unconditional love would allow Marsha's mother to punish her for her wrongdoing but it would not stop her from hugging her child, from talking and communicating with her child, from pointing out the good qualities of her child—all of this in an attempt to not allow the punishment to bruise the self-esteem and the delicate, developing, psyche of her child.

In many Haitian households, parents cut off communication with a child sometimes for long periods of time because of something the child has done. Nothing could be more detrimental to the mind of a growing child. When a parent stops talking to a child, rest assured that non-verbal communication is still taking place. The parent's attitude and body language make the child feel ignored, ashamed, unimportant, and worthless. In those particular households, this is often worsened by extra attention paid to other siblings. Jealousy, envy, and even hatred are all feelings that the child can now begin to direct toward the siblings. When parents do not acknowledge or engage a child verbally, they send the nonverbal message that the child is only worth speaking to or worth loving when he does what the parents think is right. They leave him no room for mistakes and this child comes to understand that parental love is therefore conditional.

Conditional love places an overwhelming burden on the child which can only result in destructive patterns. One possibility is that the child will become terrified of making mistakes. Some of these children will attempt to become perfectionists—an impossible task that only creates more frustration and heartache.

Another way children react to conditional love is by giving up altogether. After unsuccessfully attempting many times to please the parents, children begin to experience feelings of hopelessness. They begin to realize that they can never reach the impractical expectations imposed on them. This is very dangerous for children because it is during those times that they begin to look for people outside of the household who value them for the human beings that they are. They begin to search for people whose expectations they actually are able to meet. The conditional love of parents actually makes it a world easier for children to fall into the arms of strangers who may not truly have their best interests at heart.

Conditional love ruins a child's positive self-esteem. In *Self-Esteem: A Family Affair*, Jean Illsley Clarke explains positive self-esteem as everything that enables the child to be strong, capable, competent and positive. A child with a positive self-esteem has no doubt of his parents' love. He is never confused by their actions because explanation and clarification are never lacking. This child takes responsibility for his actions and understands that his fate rests in his own hands. The confidence he has gained from his parents allows him to encounter any problem head on and deal effectively with consequences.

Our children look up to us to be their greatest fans. They expect us to pick them up and to be there for them through thick and thin. When we empower our children and show them how important they are, we progressively narrow the window of opportunity for outside negative forces to influence them. This has tremendous implications on the adults they become later on in life. Children who receive conditional love only learn to return the same but when we love our children unconditionally, we give them the ability to positively impact their families. When stronger families are built, stronger communities become possible and from stronger communities we find all the elements necessary to build stronger nations. The future of our country depends on the types of children we raise.

Haiti needs people who know how to love and know how to lead. Regardless of what we learn in school or in our travels, many of the basic characteristics of great leaders and responsible human beings are learned at a very young age—and they are taught at home by mommy and daddy.

15

Just Do it!

I remember how I felt when my maternal grandmother died. Ever since she left New York in 1999 to return home, I promised myself that I would find a way to visit her. She did not return to Haiti in the best of health having been diabetic for many years. In fact, when she went back, after having had an operation that removed one of her eyes, although no one said it out loud, we all knew that there was a good chance we would never see her again in New York. Circumstances being what they were, we said our goodbyes and promised that we would visit her. I really meant to keep my promise.

There seemed to be no time between 1999 and 2002 that was appropriate or feasible for me to make a trip to Haiti. Somehow, life always seemed too busy—there were always too many obligations. I never did make the trip. I never saw my grandmother alive again.

I never got to tell her how much I appreciated her years of laboring on the farm, in the rocky mountains of Haiti. She contributed greatly to my having an easy life as a child. I never got to tell her how I loved watching her play with my children. I never got to tell her how important and great it made me feel to be the recipient of her unconditional love. I never did get to tell her how much I loved her back and wished that I could be half the woman she was.

In retrospect, this was a trip I could have easily made on a weekend. Although the time never seemed right, I wish I had found a way to make it. I wish I had just done it.

Safely tucked in between the pages of a manual are two greetings cards I purchased in 1998. The recipients were to be my two best childhood friends. I had fallen out of touch with both of them and was missing them greatly. One was my church friend, the one who never judged and yet always advised. The one I got in trouble for writing notes to during my father's sermons—the one who knew all of my insecurities as a young girl.

The other was my best friend from school. We walked to school together every single morning of the week. It was preferable to face old men exposing themselves to us in abandoned parked cars or at the subway station, rather than ride the dreadful school bus. She introduced me to Puerto Rican cuisine which, to this day, my ample hips still have to thank her for. She was my crazy and daring pal. If my church friend was the one I completely identified with, the one that I could see every bit of myself in, then my school friend was the person I loved but would never have the guts to become.

I purchased the identical cards in 1998 for both of them. The other day, while leafing through the pages of the manual for a research project, I found them and my heart sank. I wish I had just mailed them out in 1998. That would have saved me the pain I feel years later when I realize that I can count on one hand the number of times I have talked to either one of them in the past few years.

I use personal examples to show how important it is to follow our instincts and resist procrastination. Leaving things undone or unsaid is one of the greatest roadblocks to our success. The price of idleness can be too great to bear.

I love Nike's *"just do it"* slogan. It sends the message that we are to be about business. We are not to overly stress ourselves, however, to chronically leave our work undone or to always leave for tomorrow things we can do today is both foolish and self limiting.

Sometimes we procrastinate for what seem to be very good reasons. Particularly when it comes to Haiti, we may not be totally sure how our work might be received or if anyone would even care to join us. It is understandable to experience fear but it is not wise to allow that fear to consume us to the point of being stuck. Whatever it is you feel you could do for yourself and your country, waste no more time being afraid, waste no more energy worrying about what people will say and just do it. I borrow the following poem from Mother Teresa:

Anyway

People are often unreasonable, illogical, and self centered
Forgive them anyway.

If you are kind, people may accuse you of selfish, ulterior motives
Be kind anyway.

*If you are successful, you will win some false
friends and some true enemies
Succeed anyway.*

*If you are honest and frank, people may cheat you
Be honest and frank anyway.*

*What you spend years building, someone could
destroy overnight
Build anyway.*

*If you find serenity and happiness, they may be
jealous
Be happy anyway.*

*The good you do today, people will often forget
tomorrow
Do good anyway.*

*Give the world the best you have, and it may never
be enough
Give the world the best you've got anyway.*

*You see, in the final analysis, it is between you and
God,
It was never between you and them anyway.*

16

There is Hope!

In the course of writing this book, I came across many setbacks. There were days when I became so discouraged that I just would not write. The reports from Haiti are never encouraging. Some days I convinced myself that our situation could not get any worse. I felt that our case was truly hopeless. It was difficult to keep writing about hope when every waking day brought with it new obstacles.

It was always during those times that I would bump into someone like my neighbor, Frantz Minuty. I've never met a prouder Haitian than Frantz and I've always been amazed at how humble he is about his accomplishments and contributions to Haiti. Unbeknownst to him, Frantz always allowed me to see that there is still hope. However weakly its flame burns, Haiti's torch is still lit. Someone is always carrying it and we only have to join in.

We have to feel motivated when we remember the kind of people we are. We have always been able to eke out our existence amid the greatest of adversities. We have survived some of the greatest insults imaginable and yet we are still here.

I remember farmers who, year after year, worked at the land with little more than their bare hands and always harvested plenty. I remember my grandfather rising early and leaving his home while it was still dark outside. I can still see him grabbing his *macoute*[3] and I don't know what he did to care for the animals and I'm not really sure what his strategy was for working the land, but the fresh milk he brought home to us every morning and the fresh vegetables we ate every day were absolutely priceless.

I remember healthy Haitian women who worked from the rising of the sun to its setting with the strength of a thousand horses. They walked mile after mile to the marketplace to sell their goods, after having walked mile after mile to the river to get fresh water—and I'm not sure of the kind of days they had but I know at the end of each, they again walked mile after mile back home to cook for and take care of their families.

I remember our artists gifted as any others under the sun—the production of their bare hands being sold at a premium all over the world while they take in pennies for their creative license—but I see them, still existing, still pursuing, still hoping that the gold mine on which they sit will someday materialize.

I can't help but think of our gifted musicians, writers, teachers and countless others who have brought us national pride. They continue to exist despite the odds. They hold our country in high esteem and create hope.

I see us as a people rich in culture and tradition with a strong desire to survive. In spite of what we are told and what we have witnessed, we still have the guts to push forward; we still have the nerves of steel and the tenacity to hang on. I heard a man on television the other day say that the fact we are still talking about an existing Haiti is evidence of the strength and character of its people. In spite of all we have encountered, we continue to exist and we continue to dream and work for better days.

There has to be hope for the many who have sacrificed themselves for our cause. There has to be hope for our children. We can accomplish unbelievable goals if we really want to. As long as we are alive and have love for

our country there has to be hope.

---

[3] *A large work sack used by farmers.*

Appendix

Following are addresses and other contact information for various charitable organizations:

Beyond Borders
Jonathan Haggard, Co-Director
P.O. Box 2132
Norristown, PA 19404
Phone: (610)277-5045
www.beyondborders.net
Email: mail@beyondborders.net

Circles of Change-- Participatory Learning & Leadership in Haiti
John Engle
P.O. Box 337
Hershey, PA 17033
Phone: 202-236-6532
Email: john@johnengle.net
http://circlesofchange.com

Clean Water for Haiti
Pierre Payen, Haiti
Phone: (country code) + 509-547-3210
Website: www.cleanwaterforhaiti.org
Email: info@cleanwaterforhaiti.org

Dorsainvil Foundation
P. O Box 7896
Delray Beach Fl 33482-7896
Phone 561-279-0991, Fax 561-279-0539

Echod'Haiti.com
P.O. Box 261
Olney, MD 20830
Email : info@echodhaiti.com
WWW.echodhaiti.com

Fonkoze
Anne H. Hastings, Director
Avenue Jean Paul II, #7 (à l'interieur) Port-au-Prince, Haiti
Phone: (509) 221-7631, 7641, 513-7631
Fax: (509) 221-7520
Phone from the U.S. (800) 293-0308
Email: director@fonkoze.org

Fonkoze USA
John R. Mercier, CFE
Executive Director, Florida Office
4186 Moss Oak Place
Sarasota, FL 34231
Phone (941)921-5626
Email: jmercier@fonkoze.org

Friends of the Children of Haiti (FOTCOH)
Eric Behrens - President
4007 Smithville Rd.
Bartonville, IL 61607
Phone: 309-697-6473
Haiti
Rue FOTCOH #1
Cyvadier, Haiti
Phone: 309-282-4871

Haitian Health Foundation
Jeremiah J. Lowney, Jr., President
Marilyn Lowney, Executive Director
97 Sherman Street
Norwich, CT 06360
(860) 886-4357
www.haitianhealthfoundation.org

Konbit Sante
Elizabeth Cheatham, MA, MPH, Operations Manager
PO Box 11281
Portland, ME 04104
Phone: 207-347-6733

Lambi Fund of Haiti
Karen Ashmore, Executive Director
PO Box 18955
Washington DC 20036
Phone: 202-833-3713
Josette Perard, Haiti Director
#94 Avenue Lamartinière
Port-au-Prince, Haiti
Phone: (509) 245-9445
Email: info@lambifund.org
www.lambifund.org

North Haiti Mission
c/o Rev. Verdieu Laroche
957 River street
Hyde Park MA, 02136
E-mail: dlar@juno.com
WWW.NORTHHAITIMISSION.ORG

Oasis for Children, Inc.
Luceanna Altino-Moore, President
P.O. Box 5231
Somerset NJ, 08874-5231
Phone: 732-227-0845, 908-208-1311
Fax: 732-227-0846
Email: lucem30@hotmail.com or godsoasis@hotmail.com

ODEVTHOLAB (Oganization pour le Développement de Thomassin Laboule)
146-09 227th street
Rosedale, NY 11413
Email: odevtholab@yahoo.com
Phone: (718)775-2437

Partners in Progress
Dr. Richard A. Gosser
329 N. Fairfield Street
Ligonier, PA 15658
Phone: (724) 238-9204, (724) 875-2899
Fax: (724) 238-4603
Email: rgosser@PIPHaiti.org, or info@PIPHaiti.org
www.PIPHaiti.org

Sun Ovens International, Inc.
Paul M. Munsen
39 W 835 Midan Drive
Elburn, IL 60119
Web site: www.sunoven.com
E-mail: paul@sunoven.com
Phone: 630-208-7273, 800-408-7919
Fax: 630-208-7386

Windows on Haiti
Guy S. Antoine
35 Fairview Avenue
South Orange, NJ 07079
Phone: 973-761-0467
http://haitiforever.com
http://windowsonhaiti.com

Yéle Haiti Foundation
PO Box 2345
New York, NY 10108
Phone: (212) 352-0552 (voicemail only)

WWW.yele.org

Bibliography

Beatrice-Hall, Evelyn (S. G. Tallentyre). "The Friends of Voltaire," (University Press of the Pacific, 2003).

Clarke, Jean Illsley. "Self-Esteem: A Family Affair," (Minnesota: Hazelden 1998), 7-11.

Covey, Stephen. "The Seven Habits of Highly Effective People: Restoring the Character Ethic," (G. K. Hall & Co., 1997).

Dyer, Wayne. "Wisdom of Ages," (HarperCollins Canada / Harper Trade; 1st edition, 1998).

Keller, Helen. "The story of my life," (New York: Bantam Books, 1990).

Kimbro, Dennis and Hill, Napoleon. "Think and Grow Rich: A Black Choice," (New York: Ballantine Books, 1991).

Mother Teresa. "A Simple Path," (New York: Ballantine Books, 1995), 185.

Ross, Campbell. "Relational Parenting", (Chicago: Moody Press, 2000), 12

Robbins, Stephen. "Organizational behavior: Concepts, Controversies, Applications," (New Jersey: Prentice Hall; 8th edition, 1998)

Sheets, Buddy "The Importance of Little Things,"
http://www.passionforjesus.org/theimportanceoflittl
ethings.htm, 2005.

Maryse Aurelus-Nelson was born in Haiti in 1969. In 1980, she left her grandmother, Victoire Clermont, to join her parents in Brooklyn, New York. She attended New York University and in 1991, graduated with a Bachelor's degree in Physical Therapy. In 2000, she obtained a Master's degree in Business Administration from the University of Phoenix. Today, Maryse lives with her family in Kissimmee, Florida.

www.ingramcontent.com/pod-product-compliance
Lightning Source LLC
Chambersburg PA
CBHW030016290326
41934CB00005B/364